NEXT STEP

DISCOVER CHURCH

*Next Steps ... Empowering You
to Discover a God-Imagined Life*

Written by Lee Anderson

DISCOVER CHURCH: Next Steps

© Copyright 2012 - Discover Church

Discover Church can be contacted at dchurch.tv/
or P.O. Box 431, Avon, OH 44011

Published by TrueNorth Ink (truenorthpublish.com)

For worldwide distribution. Printed in the U.S.A.

CONTENTS

IT'S ABOUT THE HEART

You just made a decision that will radically affect your life forever. Your prayer to surrender your life to Jesus results in a brand new life and an eternity to enjoy relationship with the One who imagined and created you.

This short book will guide you through your next steps in fully realizing a *God-Imagined Life* in every way ...

> ➤ Physically

> ➤ Emotionally

> ➤ Relationally

> ➤ Spiritually

I encourage you to read through this booklet in one sitting, right now. Then, over the next several days, take a single section each day, and review the scriptures and concepts presented. I believe it will start you on a strong path to develop an understanding of your relationship with the Lord and in growing your faith.

A PARABLE

Jesus told the following story about a farmer who went out to sow his seed in the field. This story is called a parable – a story made up to illustrate key points or ideas.

> *"Listen! A farmer went out to plant some seeds. As he scattered them across his field, some seeds fell on a footpath, and the birds came and ate them. Other seeds fell on shallow soil with underlying rock. The seeds sprouted quickly because the soil was shallow. But the plants soon wilted under the hot sun, and since they didn't have deep roots, they died. Other seeds fell among thorns that grew up and choked out the tender plants. Still other seeds fell on fertile soil, and they produced a crop that was thirty, sixty, and even a hundred times as much as had been planted! Anyone with ears to hear should listen and understand" (Matt. 13:3-9).*

After telling this story, Jesus explained what it meant to his disciples, those who were closest to him. Remember, he told the story for a specific reason, and he wanted them to understand what each part of it meant.

SEED ON THE FOOTPATH

The first kind of seed fell on the footpath, the common ground where people walk. The birds came and ate it.

The seed couldn't grow or take root.

Jesus said this represents people who hear the message of faith but don't understand. The message of Jesus doesn't take root in their lives because the soil is hard and compacted: their hearts were hard and their minds were not willing to hear.

SHALLOW SOIL

Some of the seed fell on soil that was really shallow.

Jesus said this represents people who hear and respond, but the message doesn't take root in their lives. When problems happen or other distractions occur, they move away from their decision and fall away.

THORNY SOIL

Some of the seed fell on soil with lots of thorn bushes in it.

The message of Jesus connected in people's hearts, but then, the worries of life and the greed for money and material things pushed past the decision to live a *God-Imagined Life*. These people end up giving up.

FERTILE SOIL

The last kind of soil is the kind that allows the seed to grow. It germinates, takes root and then fully develops, producing a rich crop in people's lives.

The real question is what type of soil will you be? As you continue reading and thinking, I believe the next few days will answer this question.

You can be the good soil that Jesus was talking about. Don't let your soil be contaminated with thorns or be too hard. But rather, allow your life to be ready to hear and obey what God is speaking to your heart.

And grow like crazy!

Next Steps to Advance

I want you to be that "fertile soil" that allows the seed of relationship with Jesus to grow and grow. So I want you to follow these simple steps so you can begin growing right away.

PRAY

Jesus lived his life with regular times of prayer.

He needed to connect with the Father through focused times of talking with Him, of pouring out His heart and looking for wisdom and answers to the challenges he faced. One time, Jesus spent the entire night in prayer before he decided who his leaders would be.

Prayer is just as simple as talking to a close friend or maybe a family member. It doesn't have to be fancy or formal. It just needs to be from the heart.

I would like you to start every day during this next week with a time set aside to pray. Jesus gave a great example of prayer in Matt. 6.

Our Father in heaven, may your name be kept holy ...
(an expression of worship)

May your Kingdom come soon ...
(lead my life today, I want to experience your design)

May your will be done on earth, as it is in heaven ...
(I desire what you have imagined for me)

Give us today the food we need ...
(provide for my needs today)

And forgive us our sins ...
(forgive me again today)

As we have forgiven those who sin against us ...
(I'll forgive others as well)

And don't let us yield to temptation, but rescue us from the evil one. ...
(lead me and keep me from things that will tempt me)

Use the above prayer as a road map for the next seven days.

Start with some simple worship, then ask for guidance for the day. You can follow the way Jesus prayed or use your own words. But take time to pray every day.

Start your day by talking with the One who imagined you.

READ

The Bible gives a simple and direct command to those who follow him. Think about the following verse:

Don't copy the behavior and customs of this world, but let God transform you into a new person by changing the way you think (Rom. 12:2a).

How do we "learn" to change the way we think? By being a student. To listen, to study, to understand – all of these efforts help us to grow and can change the way we think.

Here is the reality: if you will study, God's Spirit will help you to understand, to change and to discover a *God-Imagined Life.* That is exactly what the 2nd part of this verse says…

Then you will learn to know God's will for you, which is good and pleasing and perfect (Rom. 12:2b).

The last part of this book gives you a study lesson for each day of the next week. I encourage you to read a section each day. I created seven days of devotionals and follow-up questions for you to read and consider. Take a few minutes each day and read the scripture and answer the questions.

LISTEN

My life is pretty busy. I'll bet yours is to.

Yet it's important you take time to quiet yourself and listen to what God is speaking to your life each day. I know that if you will take time to listen, God will speak to you and you'll be amazed at how you will grow in your faith and understanding.

Each morning, after you have taken a few minutes to pray, just quiet yourself and listen. It's hard to hear with all the stuff going on in our lives, so don't be so busy and clutter up the moment.

Just be still for a few minutes and listen. You will be amazed at how you will grow.

CONNECT WITH DC

One of the ways to grow in your faith is to connect with Discover Church. I want you to hear the messages and teachings we provide. I want you to connect with other people at DC. You can do that in our *Discover Community* groups, through different activites, and even through building some connections with people in DC on your own.

Invite someone to coffee and spend a few minutes sharing your story with someone at DC. Be an active part of the community because that is part of who we are as a church.

The DC Story

My wife, Cori and I, started Discover Church to connect with people who weren't connected anywhere else.

There are lots of churches in our area, and many are really great communities. I have very close friendships with pastors of some of those churches. So, why do we need another church? Because, I believe God is working in the lives of people like you, and He will use DC to help you grow, connect and realize the kind of life He has imagined for you all along.

I don't mean to imply that your life will be easy from this point forward. I'm not promising that everything will always work out in simple and predictable ways. I'm not going to promise that you'll get rich, or become famous or that every problem in your life will be solved.

But I will promise you this ... there is no better way to live!

I've been walking with Jesus for a long time – since I was a kid.

My parent's raised me in church. From the time I was a little boy, some of my earliest memories are about being in church. But I somehow understood the difference between going to church and having a relationship with Jesus. My parents were able to help me understand the difference – my faith was not about going to church but about having a relationship with the One who made me.

That relationship became even more important when I lost my father at a young age in my pre-teen years. The loss of my dad had an unexpected outcome. I became even more dependent on my relationship with Father God. When I would have looked to my dad for direction or support, I instead looked to God.

My faith and confidence grew. Over the years I have come to the conclusion there is just no better way to live than in right relationship with the One who imagined me and everything around me. Absolutely everything.

Cori and I have five children. It's amazing how parenthood shapes your life and challenges you to grow and adapt. How is it that each child can be so different? They are raised by the same parents, in the same home, with the same kind of food, the same water to drink and even breathing the same air.

But each child is so different from their siblings: different personalities, different looks, different talents and abilities. Just different!

Yet as a dad, I love them each uniquely. I can't say that I love one more than the other, yet I love them each in a unique way.

If I can do that with my five kids, think about how God loves you, me and the other nearly seven billion people on the planet uniquely. That is the key! Father loves you so much and He has a unique interest in your life, how you live, what you do and who you can influence.

I am convinced that God never does anything in our lives just for us! We want to believe that is the case, but I don't believe it's true. He has the amazing ability to work in my life, for me and my benefit, but not exclusively for me.

In other words, it's not just about me!

God reached you through Discover Church - for you, but also for others in your life.

I want you to tell "your world" what Jesus has done in your life. I want them to hear about this amazing sense of love and acceptance that you are experiencing. I want you to tell everyone you know how Jesus has forgiven you and how you now have relationship with the God who created everything that has ever been or ever will be.

Discover Church is not just for you. It's also for those in your life. In the same manner that God reached you through someone who knew you and invited you to DC, He wants to reach others in your life through you. Who can you invite? Who can you share your story with?

Your God-Imagined Life

Why does Discover Church exist?

The simple answer is ... *To Help People Discover a God Imagined Life through faith in Jesus Christ.*

So what does a *God-Imagined Life* look like?

First, it means realizing purpose ... what God has imagined for you, for your family and for those whom you influence.

Second, it means finding a deep sense of fulfillment in your life. There is no greater sense of peace and comfort in this life than to live each day in relationship with God. Living in the purpose He has imagined for you and and walking in relationship releases an incredible sense of fulfillment.

Third, you can realize God's love and acceptance. Before you prayed to invite Jesus into your heart and life there was a separation between you and God. Your sin caused that separation. But now, you are forgiven and there is no more separation.

You can live everyday with the confidence of realizing and experiencing God's love and acceptance.

DAILY DEVOTIONAL

Day 1 ... New Creation

This means that anyone who belongs to Christ has become a new person. The old life is gone; a new life has begun! (2 Cor. 5:17).

What a beautiful statement. Anyone who belongs to Jesus – anyone! That means you and that means me. It's the clean slate. It's the "do-over."

I love watching movies. One of my favorites is *City Slickers* starring Billy Chrystal. It's a story about three middle-aged friends who go on a cattle drive in another futile attempt to prove they're still young.

The story captures my attention as one of the friends comes to realize his life is a complete wreck. Divorce impending, breakup of the family, loss of job, life was a mess in every possible way.

His friend looks him in the eye and says, "It's a do-over." What was that? "A do-over. You know, when we were kids and you threw the ball and missed. We yelled, "Do-over!"

That is what Jesus offers to you and me. "A do-over." It's the chance to do it again. Free from the cost of past sin. It's a chance to start over, to know we can be forgiven.

And we can now forgive ourselves too! That is the key. Jesus has forgiven you. Father God no longer remembers your sin. Now, can you embrace the "do-over?"

Study Questions:

➢ Can you forgive yourself?

➢ If you struggle with that, take a few minutes to write down what you need to forgive yourself for.

➢ Is there anybody else that you need to ask forgiveness from?

Day 2 ... Reasonable Sacrifice

And so, dear brothers and sisters, I plead with you to give your bodies to God because of all he has done for you. Let them be a living and holy sacrifice—the kind he will find acceptable. This is truly the way to worship him (Romans 12:1).

Once a very religious person asked Jesus, "What do I need to do to please God?" Jesus said, "Love the Lord your God with all of your heart, all of your soul, all of your strength and all of your mind."

What does God want from you today? Make no mistake, He wants all of you.

➢ He wants **all of your heart** – your intention and motivation in life.

➢ He wants **all of your soul** – your intellect and your thoughts.

➢ He wants **all of your might** – all of your strength and all of your power.

Does that mean God wants them for himself? No, but He does want all you do to honor Him and acknowledge Him.

Why?

It's pretty simple really. He has always imagined a kind of life for you. He wants you to live well, to live free, to live in integrity, to live in honesty, to live free from the baggage of what sin creates in our lives.

By following Him in how you live, you avoid the consequences.

Follow what God has imagined in your marriage – you can build a strong and healthy marriage. Follow what God has imagined for your family – you'll enjoy a strong relationship with your family. Live with integrity in your life – you'll enjoy a good name and the trust of others.

Live your life today as a reasonable sacrifice in everything you do, what you say, how you think. Honor God and realize a *God-Imagined Life* today.

Study Questions:

➢ What area of your life do you need to work on in giving a sacrifice today?

➢ How can you honor God with your life today?

Day 3 ... God's Imagination

> *No eye has seen, no ear has heard, and no mind has imagined*
> *what God has prepared for those who love him (1 Cor. 2:9).*

Imagination. It could be one of the greatest gifts God gave to humanity: the ability to imagine.

Think about it. Any creation that humankind has ever made began with an idea.

Our greatest systems of government, the most moving storyline in a book or a movie, the most delicious dessert you have ever tasted – all began with an idea.

Someone had to imagine what the outcome would be. They had to begin with a completed idea using their imagination and then, only working from that concept, they proceeded to bring their imagined thought into reality. The sculptor begins with imagination. The musician begins with a mental musical idea – their imagination.

The Bible tells us this amazing promise: we, in all of our ability to imagine what could be, cannot even begin to consider what God has imagined for us that love Him.

Father has imagined such great things regarding you and me that we can't even conceive it. That's quite an imagination, because I have to be honest, I could imagine some really great things regarding my future. Perhaps that is also the problem.

You see, when we think about our imagined future, it pretty much revolves around us or our families – those that are closest to us. The key difference is that when God imagines what He has in store for us, it always involves the greater purpose and plan of not just us, but so many others around us.

This is the great promise of God's imagination working in our lives.

Study Questions:

➢ What have you imagined for your life and in your future?

➢ Are you willing to give those dreams and imaginations to God and allow Him to direct your life now? Even if that means giving up what you have imagined?

Day 4 ... Repentance

*But if we confess our sins to him, he is faithful and just to
forgive us our sins and to cleanse us from all wickedness
(1 John 1:9).*

There is an old saying that you may have heard, "Confession is
good for the soul." It is a simple but direct truth that holds true
for the human condition. When we confess our failures, our sins,
and our wrongdoings, we are reconciled to one another and to
ourselves.

We can face the truth of our own failure.

The word *repentance* is similar to confession, but its more. Confession is the admission. When the little boy is caught with the
cookie in his hand and is asked by a parent, "Did you take the
cookie from the cookie jar?" The child's first instinct is more than
likely to deny it, but after some coaxing from the parent, the child
finally admits or confesses. He acknowledges he took the cookie
even when mommy or daddy had told him not to.

Repentance goes beyond confession.

It is not only acknowledging that we took the cookie, but also
the recognition that it was wrong and we don't want to repeat it.

Our great challenge is, it's not that simple! We can decide we
won't repeat it again, but so often we do. That is why we depend
on the power of the Holy Spirit. We are not alone in this journey!

Here is the beautiful thing. The verse that you read from 1 John
was written to those who were walking with Jesus already. It is
the solution to my problem and to yours. I am forgiven, and I can
continue to be forgiven – that is the work of Christ. He forgives
me for my yesterday and my tomorrow.

Study Questions:

➢ Are there any sin issues; behaviors or patterns that you need to confess and repent of today?

➢ If there are, James 5:16 encourages us to confess those faults to others so we can be healed. Find someone today that you can confess to. Someone who shares your faith and you can trust.

Day 5 ... The Power of Holy Spirit

> *So I say, let the Holy Spirit guide your lives. Then you won't be doing what your sinful nature craves. (Gal. 5:16).*

Jesus clearly told his disciples, it would be best if he went away so that the Holy Spirit would come. That was the plan, so we could live each day relying on the Holy Spirit to help us and empower us.

Think about it. God's Spirit is living in YOU! What a mind-blowing concept.

In the Apostle Paul's letter to the New Testament Church in Rome, he admitted that he struggled to do what he should. In fact, in Romans 7 he writes about the struggle we all face. Our hearts are transformed but we still struggle to do what we believe God wants us to do.

So how do we live each day? The answer is simple and direct. If we live our life, each day, listening to and following what the Holy Spirit speaks into our lives, we can realize the best that God has imagined for us.

So today, be listening to how the Holy Spirit will direct you to live.

Look for an opportunity to share your story. Be watching for the moment when the Holy Spirit brings something to your attention or asks you to do something for someone else. Today, when temptation comes your way, look for the Holy Spirit to provide a way out.

Study Questions:

> ➤ How do you "hear" or "sense" the Holy Spirit speaking into your life? An impression, a thought, through something you read? Maybe through what someone says to you or what you hear on the radio or TV?

> ➤ Will you be brave enough to step out in your new faith and act?

Day 6 ... The Power of Community

Let us think of ways to motivate one another to acts of love and good works. And let us not neglect our meeting together, as some people do, but encourage one another, especially now that the day of his return is drawing near (Heb. 10:24-25).

God never imagined that you and I would need to walk the journey of our life alone. In fact, he designed the church to be part of the solution so that we could live out our lives in community with others who share our faith.

This is what Discover Church is all about. Creating community that walks the journey together. Our Discover Community groups are "doing life together" by building friendships, learning together, praying together, and sharing life experience with others.

Community can provide encouragement, inspiration and a helping hand. With genuine friendships, we learn best, live healthy and keep balance in our lives.

I recognize that being part of a church community takes some discipline. As we meet on Sunday mornings or other times, there are lots of things you could do with your time. But can those things really replace the power of community?

That is why the Bible encourages us to remain part of the church community. Don't neglect your participation and role at DC. We need you, and you need us.

Study Questions:

- What are you learning at Discover Church?

- How has the DC community inspired you in your faith or in your life?

Day 7 ... The Grace of God

God saved you by his grace when you believed. And you can't take credit for this; it is a gift from God. Salvation is not a reward for the good things we have done, so none of us can boast about it (Eph. 2:8-9).

Let's face it. I didn't deserve God's forgiveness. You didn't earn God's favor in your life. We can't be good enough, smart enough, and religious enough to warrant God's mercy. It is His gift of love.

So don't try to earn it!

What I mean is this, don't fall into the trap of thinking that now you have experienced forgiveness and are walking in relationship with Jesus, you can try to earn His favor by being better. Or doing good enough!

Instead, focus on obeying His direction in your life each day. When you make mistakes, acknowledge it, repent, forgive yourself and move on. God's grace is there everyday, and it's new every day!

I want you to understand this. As your faith grows, so does your tendency to be self-reliant. As you learn more, you become more confident. As your life changes, you will begin to realize the kind of life God imagined for you, and you will have greater confidence in yourself.

If you're not real careful, suddenly you're relying more on yourself than you are on God.

Here's the bottom line – you will make mistakes. You will fail! So walk in God's grace, keeping your heart soft before Him. Love Him with all of your heart, soul, strength and mind.

Study Questions:

> ➤ What does God's grace mean to you today?

> ➤ Are you trying to "be good" on your own strength? If so, what is an example?

INFO

Want to learn more about Discover Church?
Check out our online resources at:

www.dchurch.tv

or at Facebook: www.facebook.com/dchurch.tv

Pastor Lee Anderson has lived in Northeastern Ohio for
more than twenty years. He and his wife Cori are the
parents of five children and have been married
for twenty-five years. As the lead pastor for Discover
Church, he has a passion to see people realize
God's best in and through their lives.

Connect with Pastor Lee at lee.anderson@dchurch.tv
or 440-263-2153

Discover Church Mailing Address:
PO Box 431, Avon, OH 44011

Printed in Great Britain
by Amazon